CHAMELEONS ARE COOL

For my family M.J.
For Sam and Harry S.S.

First published 1997 by Walker Books Ltd
87 Vauxhall Walk, London SE11 5HJ

This edition published 2010

2 4 6 8 10 9 7 5 3 1

Text © 1997 Martin Jenkins
Illustrations © 1997 Sue Shields

The moral rights of the author and illustrator
have been asserted

This book has been typeset in Bembo Educational

Printed in China

British Library Cataloguing in Publication Data:
a catalogue record for this book is available from the British Library

ISBN 978-1-4063-1857-9

www.walker.co.uk

CHAMELEONS ARE COOL

Martin Jenkins

illustrated by
Sue Shields

WALKER BOOKS
AND SUBSIDIARIES
LONDON · BOSTON · SYDNEY · AUCKLAND

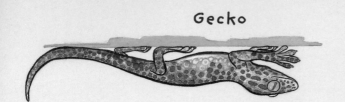

Gecko

Some lizards eat bananas –
chameleons don't.
Some lizards walk upside down
on the ceiling –
chameleons can't.

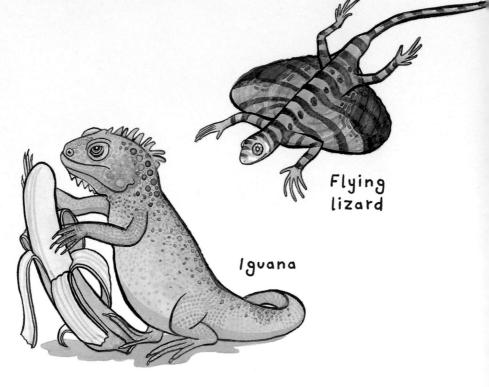

Flying
lizard

Iguana

4

There's even a lizard that glides
from tree to tree –
a chameleon certainly
wouldn't do that!

But of all the different kinds of lizard,
I still think chameleons are the best.
Chameleons are cool.

Chameleon

It's not that they're all that big.
The biggest is only about
the size of a rather small cat.
It's called Oustalet's
chameleon and it lives in
Madagascar.

They can be
really really
small, though.

The smallest one could
balance happily on
your little finger.
It's called the
Dwarf Brookesia,
and it lives in
Madagascar, too.

And I suppose you wouldn't exactly
call many of them beautiful.
Their skin is wrinkly and bumpy,
and they've got big, bulgy eyes,
while lots of them have
the most ridiculous …

noses!

(I think it's their noses I like best.)

Their mouths are pretty
odd, too. They turn down
at the corners, which is
why chameleons always
look grumpy.

Actually they don't just
look grumpy ...

they **are** grumpy. So if two chameleons bump into each other, things can get pretty lively. There's lots of puffing and hissing – and sometimes, there's a real fight.

And that's when chameleons do
what they're most famous for –
they change colour.

Lots of people think chameleons change
colour to match their surroundings.
They don't!
They change colour
when they're angry,

or when they're too cold or too hot,
or when they're sick.

And there are some sorts
of chameleon that hardly
change colour at all.

As a rule, though, chameleons don't bump into each other all that often. I suppose it wouldn't be fair to call them lazy, but they certainly don't move any more than they have to. And when they do, it's almost always incredibly slowly.

Sometimes they stop completely, in mid-step, as if they've quite forgotten what they're supposed to be doing.

But if you look closely you'll see that they're actually carefully peering about.

Now, peering about is something
chameleons are rather good at.
That's because their eyes can move
separately from each other,
unlike our eyes which
always move
together.

So while one eye is looking back
over the chameleon's shoulder, the
other one is scanning the branches
ahead.

As soon as it spots something tasty,
the chameleon fixes both eyes
on its prey and begins to
creep forwards –
even more slowly
than usual.
Then it opens its mouth
just a crack, and ...

out shoots this amazingly long
tongue, with a sticky bit at the end,
like a piece of well-chewed
chewing gum.

thwap!

Then the tongue flies back,
and there's a lot of
chomping and chewing,
and perhaps a few bits
of insect leg fluttering
to the ground.

And after that the chameleon
just sits there for an hour or two,
doing nothing very much at all,
looking quite exhausted
(and still grumpy)
after all that
hard work.

And there
you have it.
How could you
possibly resist a
pocket-sized,
bad-tempered, colour-
changing, swivel-eyed, snail-paced,
long-tongued sharp-shooter?

If chameleons aren't cool,
then I don't know what is!

More about chameleons and other lizards

Chameleons are lizards, and lizards are reptiles, like snakes, crocodiles and tortoises. There are about 4,000 kinds of lizard altogether, including around 120 different chameleons.

Just over half of all the kinds of
chameleon come from Madagascar,
a big island off the east coast of
Africa. Most of the others live in
mainland Africa.

Most of a chameleon's eye is covered in skin. There's a tiny peep-hole in the middle that the chameleon sees through.

A chameleon's feet are shaped like pincers for holding on tightly to branches.

A chameleon will only fight with the same kind of chameleon as itself.

Most lizards gulp their food down without chewing it, but chameleons grind everything up thoroughly! Chameleons feed on all sorts of creepy-crawlies.
The big ones also eat small birds, mice, and even other chameleons.

Iguanas don't just eat bananas. They love all sorts of fruit.

Chameleons don't make good pets – they usually get sick and die!

The flying lizard glides on wing-like flaps of skin.

A gecko's toes are as sticky as Velcro.

Index

About the Author

Martin Jenkins is a conservation biologist, who works for agencies such as the World Wide Fund for Nature. "When I first saw chameleons in the wild in Madagascar," he recalls, "I fell in love with them at first sight. I picked one up, ever so gently, and it promptly bit me on the thumb. I still think they're wonderful, but tend to leave them alone whenever I bump into them!" Martin is also the author of *The Emperor's Egg,* winner of the TES Junior Information Book Award, and *Fly Traps! Plants that Bite Back.*

About the Illustrator

Award-winning illustrator Sue Shields has
worked on everything from posters to murals,
shop interiors, magazines, newspapers,
greetings cards and children's books.
For *Chameleons Are Cool*, she had to adapt her
use of watercolour, "to try to describe not only
their astonishing colours, but a hint of the
colours they can change to." And although
she won't give any names, she says that the
chameleons' faces kept reminding her of
people she knows!

There are 10 titles in the
READ AND DISCOVER series.
Which ones have you read?

Available from all good booksellers

www.walker.co.uk

FOR THE BEST CHILDREN'S BOOKS, LOOK FOR THE BEAR.